Design: Judith Chant and Alison Lee
Recipe Photography: Peter Barry
Jacket and Illustration Artwork: Jane Winton, courtesy of
Bernard Thornton Artists, London
Editors: Jillian Stewart and Kate Cranshaw

CLB 4262
Published by Grange Books, an imprint of Grange Books PLC,
The Grange, Grange Yard, London, SE1 3AG
© 1995 CLB Publishing, Godalming, Surrey, England.
All rights reserved
Printed and bound in Singapore
Published 1995
ISBN 1-85627-578-7

THE LITTLE BOOK · OF ·

Wok
& Stir Fry
COOKING

*The ideal introduction to cooking in
traditional oriental style.*

Grange
BOOKS

Introduction

The widespread popularity of Oriental cuisine has led to a great surge in the use of the wok in this country. A wok is a deep frying pan with rounded sides which usually comes with a domed lid. It originally comes from China and is seen all over the Far-East, where a common sight is the preparation, cooking and selling of delicious stir-fry dishes on many a street corner. This Oriental pan is a wonderfully versatile piece of equipment as it can be used not only for stir-frying, but also for deep-frying and, when fitted with a wooden trivet, for steaming. Woks have caught the imagination to such an extent that they are now widely available in many kitchen equipment shops, and not just in a few Chinatown groceries, as was the case only a few years ago.

Traditionally shaped woks are designed to be used on gas cookers. The rounded nature of the pan allows the gas flame to heat the sides, so giving a wider heat distribution and cooking the food more evenly, rather than just cooking the food on the bottom of pan. Western manufacturers, however, do make flat-bottomed woks designed especially for electric cookers, so when buying a wok for the first time you should ensure that you are buying the right type for your cooker.

Stir-frying is the extremely quick and wonderfully easy method of cooking most closely associated with the wok. A small amount of oil is heated in the wok, and the freshly prepared ingredients, which are usually cut small enough to cook quickly, are stir-fried for only a few minutes until everything is just cooked through. Stir-fried foods should never be soggy and overcooked. Vegetables, in particular, should still have a crunch to them and meat should be seared on the outside and soft and melting on the inside. Speed is the essence of stir-fry cooking, and the food should be equally speedily served. The best oil to use for stir-frying is a vegetable oil such as sunflower or peanut oil (also known as groundnut oil), and always remember to heat the wok thoroughly before the oil is added. Olive oil, butter or margarine are not suitable for stir-frying as these fats are for use at lower temperatures only and will burn if subjected to the intense heat of a wok.

The step-by-step instructions in this book explain how to stir-fry delicious Chinese-style dishes of lightly spiced meats, fish and vegetables – and even fruit desserts – in the shortest time with the minimum effort.

Sesame Chicken Wings

SERVES 8

This is an economical starter that is also good as a cocktail snack or as a light meal with stir-fried vegetables.

PREPARATION: 25 mins
COOKING: 14 mins

---

12 chicken wings
1 tbsp salted black beans
1 tbsp water
1 tbsp oil
2 cloves garlic, crushed
2 slices fresh ginger, cut into fine shreds
3 tbsps soy sauce
1½ tbsps dry sherry or rice wine
Large pinch of black pepper
1 tbsp sesame seeds
Spring onions or coriander leaves to garnish

---

1. Cut off and discard the chicken wing tips. Cut between the joint to separate the wings into two pieces.

2. Crush the beans and add the water. Leave to stand.

3. Heat the oil in a wok and add the garlic and ginger. Stir briefly and add the chicken wings. Cook, stirring, until lightly browned – about 3

Step 1 Using a knife or scissors, cut through the joint in the wings and separate them into two pieces.

minutes. Add the soy sauce and wine and cook, stirring, about 30 seconds longer. Add the soaked black beans and pepper.

4. Cover the wok tightly and allow to simmer for about 8-10 minutes. Uncover and turn the heat to high. Continue cooking, stirring until the liquid is almost evaporated and the chicken wings are glazed with sauce.

5. Remove from the heat and sprinkle on the sesame seeds. Stir to coat completely and serve. Garnish with spring onions or coriander.

Pork Spareribs with Chinese Mushrooms

SERVES 4

Spareribs served with Chinese mushrooms in a slightly hot and spicy sauce make a delicious starter or main course.

PREPARATION: 15 mins
COOKING: 20 mins

900g/2lbs pork spareribs
1 carrot, finely sliced
1 leek, finely chopped
1 bay leaf
175g/6oz dried Chinese mushrooms, soaked
    for 15 minutes in warm water and drained
1 tbsp oil
1 tsp chopped garlic
½ tsp chilli sauce
1 tbsp soy sauce
1 tbsp hoisin sauce
1 tsp wine vinegar
280ml/½ pint chicken stock
Salt and pepper

1. Cut the spareribs down the bone to separate

Step 1 Blanch the spareribs in boiling water for 1 minute.

Step 1 Remove the blanched ribs and drain well.

them. Then cut them into smaller pieces, so that they are easier to handle. In a medium-sized, flameproof casserole bring to the boil plenty of water along with the carrot, leek and bay leaf. Blanch the spareribs for 1 minute in the boiling water. Remove and drain well.

2. Cook the mushrooms in the boiling water for 10 minutes. Drain well, discarding the water.

3. Heat the oil in a wok, add the garlic, chilli sauce and the mushrooms. Fry slowly until lightly coloured.

4. Stir in the soy sauce, hoisin sauce, vinegar and stock.

5. Add the spareribs, stirring all the ingredients together well. Season with salt and pepper to taste and cook, covered, for 10 minutes.

6. Remove the lid and allow the sauce to reduce slightly. Serve piping hot.

Gado Gado

SERVES 4

This makes a very appealing starter for a dinner party based on Chinese or Indonesian dishes.

PREPARATION: 20 mins
COOKING: 30 mins

---

1 tbsp peanut oil
1 carrot, cut into thin strips
1 potato, cut into thin strips
120g/4oz green beans, trimmed
120g/4oz Chinese cabbage, shredded
120g/4oz beansprouts
½ a cucumber, cut into batons

Peanut Sauce
2 tbsps peanut oil
60g/2oz raw shelled peanuts
2 red chillies, deseeded and finely chopped, or
    1 tsp chilli powder
2 shallots, finely chopped
1 clove garlic, crushed
140ml/¼ pint water
1 tsp brown sugar
Juice of ½ lemon
Salt
90ml/3 fl oz coconut milk
Sliced hard-boiled eggs, to garnish
Sliced cucumber, to garnish

---

1. Heat a wok and add the 1 tbsp peanut oil. When hot, toss in the carrot and potato. Stir-fry for 2 minutes and add green beans and cabbage. Cook for a further 3 minutes.
2. Add the beansprouts and cucumber, and stir-fry for 2 minutes. Place in a serving dish and keep warm.
3. To make the peanut sauce, heat the wok, add the 2 tbsps peanut oil, and fry the peanuts for 2-3 minutes. Remove and drain on kitchen paper.
4. Blend or pound the chillies, shallots and garlic to a smooth paste. Grind or blend peanuts to a powder.
5. Reheat the oil and fry the chilli paste for 2 minutes.
6. Add the water, and bring to the boil. Add peanuts, brown sugar, lemon juice, and salt to taste. Stir for about 10 minutes or until the sauce is thick and add coconut milk.
7. Garnish the vegetables with slices of hard-boiled egg and cucumber, and serve with the peanut sauce.

Beef with Onions

SERVES 4
Serve this marinated beef dish with plain rice or noodles.

PREPARATION: 15 mins plus 30 minutes
     marinating
COOKING: 20 mins

460g/1lb fillet steak
1 tbsp oil
1 piece fresh ginger root, peeled and roughly
     chopped
3 onions, finely sliced
1 clove garlic, chopped
280ml/½ pint beef stock
Pinch of sugar
2 tbsps dark soy sauce
1 tsp cornflour, combined with a little water
Salt and pepper

Marinade
1 tbsp oil
1 tsp sesame oil
1 tbsp Chinese wine

---

1. Cut the fillet into very thin slices across the grain.

2. Mix together the marinade ingredients and stir in the meat. Leave to marinate for 30 minutes.

3. Heat the oil in a wok and sauté the ginger, onions and garlic until lightly browned.

4. Lift the meat out of the marinade with a slotted spoon and discard the marinade. Add

Step 5 Pour over the stock, sugar and soy sauce. Cook for 4 minutes.

the meat to the wok and stir-fry with the vegetables.

5. Pour over the stock, sugar and soy sauce. Cook for 4 minutes.

6. Add the cornflour mixture to the sauce, stirring continuously until thickened. Season with salt and pepper and serve immediately.

Step 6 Add the cornflour mixture to the wok and stir continuously until thickened.

Deep-Fried Chicken with Lemon Slices

SERVES 6
This exciting dish has quite a few ingredients, but it is well worth the effort.

PREPARATION: 30 mins
COOKING: 15 mins

1.4kg/3lbs chicken breast meat
90g/3oz cornflour
3 tbsps plain flour
1 green pepper
1 red pepper
Oil for deep-frying

Marinade
½ tsp salt
½ tbsp cooking wine
½ tbsp light soy sauce
1 tbsp cornflour
1 tbsp water
1 egg yolk
Black pepper

Sauce
3 tbsps sugar
3 tbsps lemon juice
90ml/6 tbsps light stock
½ tsp salt
2 tbsps cornflour
1 tsp sesame oil

2 lemons to garnish, thinly sliced
Chopped parsley to garnish

1. Skin the chicken. Cut into bite-sized, thin slices.

2. Mix all the marinade ingredients together and marinate the chicken in the mixture for 10 minutes.

3. Mix the cornflour and plain flour together on a plate, remove the chicken from the marinade and coat each chicken piece with the flour mixture.

4. Mix all the sauce ingredients together in a small bowl. Cut the peppers into 2.5 cm/1-inch pieces.

5. Place a wok over a high heat. Heat the oil until almost smoking. Deep-fry the chicken slices until golden brown. Remove with a slotted spoon to a heated plate. Pour off all but 1 tbsp of the oil.

6. Stir-fry the peppers until they begin to brown. Pour in the sauce and bring to the boil, stirring until thickened. Add the chicken pieces. Stir for a few more minutes.

7. Transfer to a heated serving platter, and garnish with lemon slices and chopped parsley.

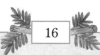

Duck with Bamboo Shoots

SERVES 4
Stir-fried bamboo shoots, served with duck breasts and a hoisin-based sauce.

PREPARATION: 10 mins
COOKING: 50 mins

225g/8oz bamboo shoots, cut into thin slices
90g/3oz sugar
140ml/¼ pint water
1 tsp chopped fresh ginger root
1 tbsp hoisin sauce
2 duck breasts
1 tbsp oil
Salt and pepper

---

1. Cook the bamboo shoots in boiling, lightly salted water for about 15 minutes. Drain thoroughly and set aside.

2. Mix the sugar and water together in a small saucepan, stirring thoroughly.

Step 3 Add the hoisin sauce to the pan. Place over a gentle heat and cook until a light syrup is formed.

Step 4 Brush the syrup liberally over the duck breasts.

3. Add the ginger and the hoisin sauce. Place over a gentle heat and cook until a light syrup is formed.

4. Brush this syrup liberally over the duck breasts.

5. Heat the oil in a wok and add the duck breasts, skin-side down first. Sear on each side. Take out and finish cooking in an oven preheated to 220°C/425°F/Gas Mark 7, for about 15 minutes.

6. Shortly before the duck breasts are cooked, stir-fry the bamboo shoots in the oil used to sear the duck breasts. Season with salt and pepper and serve hot with the sliced duck breasts. Serve any leftover sauce in a small bowl to accompany the duck.

Stir-Fried Leeks and Lamb

SERVES 4

Rosemary, redcurrant jelly and mint are all classic accompaniments to lamb and complement it perfectly.

PREPARATION: 10 mins
COOKING: 30 mins

---

1 tbsp oil
2 tsps fresh rosemary
2 tsps fresh basil leaves, chopped
460g/1lb leeks, cut into 2.5 cm/1-inch slices
460g/1lb lamb, cut into 2.5 cm/1-inch cubes
400g/14oz can plum tomatoes
1 tsp redcurrant jelly
1 tbsp chopped mint
Salt and pepper
Fresh mint to garnish

---

1. Heat a wok and add the oil. Add the rosemary, basil and leeks, and stir-fry gently for 3 minutes. Remove from the wok, and increase the heat.

2. Add the lamb and stir-fry until well-browned all over.

3. Return the leeks to the wok. Add the undrained tomatoes, redcurrant jelly, mint, and salt and pepper to taste.

4. Cover and simmer for 20 minutes, adding water if necessary. Serve hot, garnished with fresh mint.

Prawn and Scallop Stir-Fry

SERVES 4
Pine nuts and spinach give an unusual twist to this delicious dish.

PREPARATION: 35 mins
COOKING: 10 mins

3 tbsps oil
60g/4 tbsps pine nuts
460g/1lb uncooked prawns, peeled
460g/1lb shelled scallops, quartered if large
2 tsps grated fresh root ginger
1 small red or green chilli, seeded and finely
  chopped
2 cloves garlic, finely chopped
1 large red pepper, cut into 2.5 cm/1-inch
  diagonal pieces
225g/8oz fresh spinach, stalks removed and
  leaves well washed and shredded
4 spring onions, cut in 1.25 cm/½-inch diagonal
  pieces
60ml/4 tbsps fish or chicken stock
60ml/4 tbsps light soy sauce
60ml/4 tbsps rice wine or dry sherry
1 tbsp cornflour

1. Heat oil in a wok and add the pine nuts. Cook over low heat, stirring continuously until lightly browned. Remove with a draining spoon and drain on kitchen paper.

2. Add the prawns and scallops to the oil remaining in the wok and stir over a moderate heat until the scallops are beginning to look opaque and firm, and the prawns look pink.

Step 1 Cook the pine nuts in the oil until lightly browned.

3. Add the ginger, chilli, garlic and red pepper and cook a few minutes over a moderate heat.

4. Add the spinach and spring onions, and stir-fry briefly. Mix the remaining ingredients together and pour over the ingredients in the wok.

5. Turn up the heat to bring the liquid to the boil, stirring ingredients constantly. Once the liquid thickens and clears, stir in the pine nuts and serve immediately.

Step 5 Add the liquid to the pan and cook until it thickens to a sauce.

Spiced Beef

SERVES 4
This robust stir-fry dish is good served with steamed Chinese greens.

PREPARATION: 30 mins
COOKING: 5-6 mins

Marinade
1 tsp sugar
2-3 star anise, ground
½ tsp ground fennel seeds
1 tbsp dark soy sauce
¼ tsp monosodium glutamate (optional)

460g/1lb fillet of beef, cut into 2.5 cm/1-inch
    strips
2.5 cm/1-inch piece fresh root ginger, peeled
    and crushed
½ tsp salt
2 tbsps oil
4 spring onions, sliced
½ tsp freshly ground black pepper
1 tbsp light soy sauce

---

1. Mix the marinade ingredients together in a bowl.

2. Add the beef strips, ginger and salt. Stir well together to coat and marinate for 20 minutes.

3. Heat the oil in a wok. Add the spring onions and stir-fry for 1 minute.

4. Add the beef, ground pepper and the light soy sauce and stir-fry for 4-5 minutes. Serve with a dip.

Cantonese Egg Fu Yung

SERVES 2-3

As the name suggests, this dish is from Canton. However, fu yung dishes are popular in many other regions of China, too.

PREPARATION: 25 mins
COOKING: 12 mins

5 eggs
60g/2oz shredded cooked meat, poultry or fish
1 celery stick, finely shredded
4 dried Chinese mushrooms, soaked in boiling
    water for 5 minutes
60g/2oz bean sprouts
1 small onion, thinly sliced
Pinch of salt and pepper
1 tsp dry sherry
Oil for frying

Sauce
1 tbsp cornflour dissolved in 3 tbsps cold water
280ml/½ pint chicken stock
1 tsp tomato ketchup
1 tbsp soy sauce
Pinch of salt and pepper
Dash of sesame oil

1. Beat the eggs lightly and add the shredded meat and celery.

2. Squeeze all the liquid from the dried mushrooms. Discard the stems and cut the caps

Step 3 Heat the oil in a wok and spoon in 90ml/3 fl oz of the egg mixture.

into thin slices. Add to the egg mixture along with the bean sprouts and onion. Add the seasoning and sherry and stir well.

3. Heat a wok and pour in about 60ml/4 tbsps oil. When hot, carefully spoon in about 90ml/ 3 fl oz of the egg mixture.

4. Brown on one side, turn over gently and brown the other side. Remove the cooked patty to a plate and continue until all the mixture is cooked.

5. Combine all the sauce ingredients in a small, heavy-based pan and bring slowly to the boil, stirring continuously until thickened and cleared. Pour the sauce over the Egg Fu Yung to serve.

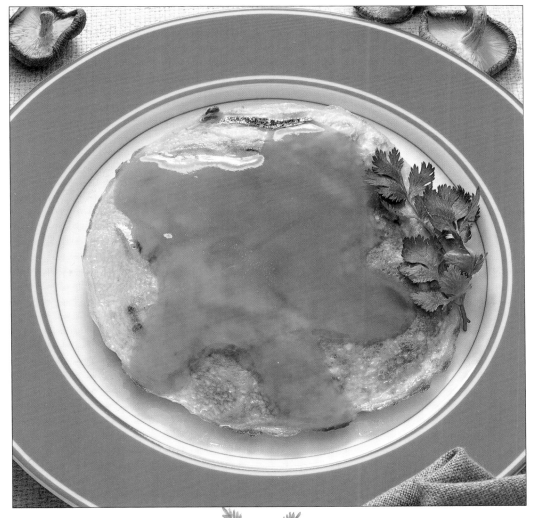

Chicken in Hot Pepper Sauce

SERVES 4
Stir-fried chicken served with peppers in a hot pepper sauce.

PREPARATION: 10 mins
COOKING: 25 mins

460-680g/1-1½lbs boned chicken meat
2 tbsps oil
1 tsp chopped garlic
1 red pepper, cut into thin strips
1 green pepper, cut into thin strips
1 tsp wine vinegar
1 tbsp light soy sauce
1 tsp sugar
280ml/½ pint chicken stock
1 tbsp chilli sauce
Salt and pepper

---

1. Cut all the chicken meat into thin strips. Heat the oil in a wok and stir-fry the garlic, chicken and the green and red peppers.

Step 1 Cut the chicken meat into thin strips.

2. Pour off any excess oil and deglaze the wok with the vinegar. Stir in the soy sauce, sugar and stock.

3. Gradually stir in the chilli sauce, tasting after each addition. Season with a little salt and pepper to taste.

4. Cook until the sauce has reduced slightly. Serve piping hot.

Beef with Tomato & Pepper in Black Bean Sauce

SERVES 4-6

*Black beans are a speciality of Cantonese cooking and give a pungent,
salty taste to stir-fried dishes.*

PREPARATION: 25 mins
COOKING: 5 mins

2 large tomatoes
2 tbsps salted black beans
2 tbsps water
60ml/4 tbsps dark soy sauce
1 tbsp cornflour
1 tbsp dry sherry
1 tsp sugar
460g/1lb rump steak, cut into thin strips
1 small green pepper
60ml/4 tbsps oil
175ml/6 fl oz beef stock
Pinch of ground black pepper

1. Core the tomatoes and cut them into

Step 1 Remove the cores from the tomatoes with a sharp knife. Cut into even-sized wedges.

Step 4 Add the beef mixture to the wok and stir-fry until the sauce thickens to glaze the meat.

wedges. Crush the black beans, add the water and set aside.

2. Combine the soy sauce, cornflour, sherry, sugar and meat in a bowl and set aside.

3. Cut the pepper into 1.25 cm/½-inch diagonal pieces. Heat a wok and add the oil. When hot, stir-fry the green pepper pieces for about 1 minute and remove.

4. Add the meat and the soy sauce mixture to the wok and stir-fry for about 2 minutes. Add the soaked black beans and the stock. Bring to the boil and allow to thicken slightly.

5. Return the pepper to the wok and add the tomatoes and black pepper. Heat through for 1 minute and serve immediately.

Sweet and Sour Pork with Pineapple

SERVES 4
This is a classic Chinese recipe that is easy to prepare at home.

PREPARATION: 15 mins
COOKING: 20 mins

460g/1lb lean pork fillet, cut into 2.5 cm/1-inch
    cubes
2 tbsps light soy sauce
2 tbsps white wine vinegar
2 tbsps tomato purée
1 tbsp sugar
2 tbsps peanut oil
1 tbsp cornflour
1 clove garlic, crushed
1 tsp grated fresh root ginger
140ml/¼ pint water
1 can pineapple pieces, drained
Fresh coriander to garnish

---

1. Place the pork in bowl, pour over the light soy sauce and toss together. Leave to marinate for 15 minutes.

2. Meanwhile, make the sauce by mixing together the vinegar, tomato purée and sugar, and set aside.

3. Heat a wok and add the oil.

4. Remove the pork from soy sauce, and add the soy to the sauce mixture. Toss the pork in the cornflour, coating well.

5. When the oil is hot, brown the pork well all over. Remove from the pan and reduce the heat.

6. Fry the garlic and ginger for 30 seconds. Add the water. Bring to the boil, then return the pork to the wok.

7. Reduce the heat; cover and simmer for 15 minutes, stirring occasionally.

8. Add the sauce mixture and pineapple, and simmer for a further 15 minutes. Garnish with coriander.

Stir-Fried Rice with Peppers

SERVES 3-4

Red and green peppers, onions and soy sauce add colour as well as flavour to this rice dish.

PREPARATION: 5 mins
COOKING: 25 mins

120g/4oz long grain rice
1 tbsp peanut oil
1 onion, chopped
1 green pepper, cut into small pieces
1 red pepper, cut into small pieces
1 tbsp soy sauce
Salt and pepper
1 tsp sesame oil

Step 3 Add the cooked rice to the wok and stir in the soy sauce.

Step 2 Heat the oil in a wok and stir-fry the onion and peppers until lightly browned.

1. Cook the rice in boiling water until just tender. Drain and set aside.

2. Heat the oil in a wok and stir-fry the onion, add the peppers and fry until lightly browned.

3. Add the rice to the wok, stir in the soy sauce and continue cooking until the rice is heated through completely.

4. Season with salt, pepper and the sesame oil and serve.

Stir-Fried Sticky Rice

SERVES 4

Glutinous rice cooked with stir-fried mushrooms, ginger and shallots makes a delicious accompaniment to a main course.

PREPARATION: 5 mins
COOKING: 25 mins

250g/9oz glutinous rice
2 tbsps oil
2 spring onions, chopped
½ onion, chopped
1 slice fresh ginger root
4 dried Chinese black mushrooms, soaked for
    15 minutes in warm water, drained and sliced
Salt and pepper

1. Wash the rice in plenty of cold water and place it in a sieve. Pour 1.3 litres/2¼ pints boiling water over the rice.

2. Heat the oil in a wok and stir-fry the spring

Step 4 Add the rice to the wok and stir in well.

Step 4 Pour in enough water to cover the rice by 1.25cm/½-inch

onions, onion and ginger until golden brown.

3. Add the mushrooms and continue cooking, stirring and shaking the wok frequently.

4. Drain the rice and add to the wok, stirring well. Pour over enough water to cover the rice by 1.25cm/½-inch.

5. Cover and cook over a moderate heat until there is almost no liquid left. Reduce the heat once again and continue cooking until all the liquid has been absorbed. This takes about 20 minutes in total.

6. Add salt and pepper to taste and serve immediately.

Peking Toffee Apples

SERVES 4
A quick and easy dessert to prepare and one which you never grow out of!

PREPARATION: 10 mins
COOKING: 20 mins

---

4 crisp apples
1 egg
60g/2oz flour
Oil for deep-frying
90g/6 tbsps sugar
3 tbsps oil
3 tbsps golden syrup

---

1. Peel, core and thickly slice the apples.

2. Blend the egg, flour and 60ml/4 tbsps water to make a smooth batter.

3. Place oil for deep-frying in a wok and heat to a moderate temperature, about 180°C/350°F.

4. Dip the apple slices in the batter just before frying. Deep-fry several slices at a time, for 2-3 minutes or until golden. Drain on kitchen paper and keep warm.

5. Heat the sugar, oil and 2 tbsps water in a pan over a low heat, until the sugar dissolves. Turn up the heat and cook for about 5 minutes until the sugar starts to caramelise. Stir in the

syrup and heat for a further 2 minutes.

6. Add the fried apple and stir slowly, covering each piece with syrup.

7. Quickly spoon hot, syrup-covered apples into a large bowl of iced water to harden syrup. Remove quickly and serve.

Step 6 Add the fritters to the syrup.

Step 7 Quickly spoon the syrup-covered apples into a large bowl of iced water to harden the syrup. Remove quickly and serve.

Stir-Fried Fruit Salad

SERVES 4

In this unusual fruit salad, the exotic ingredients are stir-fried in a little oil and delicately flavoured with cinnamon.

PREPARATION: 30 mins
COOKING: 10 mins

4 slices fresh pineapple
1 grapefruit
2 pears
1 pawpaw
1 mango
12 lychees, peeled
2 tbsps oil
2 tbsps sugar
Ground cinnamon

1. Cut off the pineapple skin and cut the flesh into thin slices. Peel the grapefruit and cut into segments. Peel the pears, the pawpaw and mango, and cut the flesh into thin slices.

Step 1 Cut the pineapple into slices. Peel and segment the grapefruit. Peel and slice the pears, pawpaw and mango.

2. Heat the oil and stir-fry the fruit in the following order: pineapple, lychees, mango, pawpaw, pears and lastly the grapefruit.

3. Sprinkle with the sugar. Cook for a few more minutes and sprinkle with the cinnamon. Serve either hot or cold.

Sweet Bean Wontons

SERVES 6

Wonton snacks, either sweet or savoury, are a popular tea house treat in China.
Made from prepared wonton wrappers and ready-made bean paste, these
couldn't be more simple.

PREPARATION: 20 mins
COOKING: 20 mins

15 wonton wrappers
225g/8oz sweet red bean paste
1 tbsp cornflour
60ml/4 tbsps cold water
Oil for deep-frying
Honey

1. Take a wonton wrapper in the palm of your hand and place a little of the red bean paste slightly above the centre.

Step 4 Pull the sides together and stick together with the cornflour and water paste.

Step 5 Turn the wonton parcels inside out by pushing the filled portion through the middle.

2. Mix together the cornflour and water and moisten the edge around the filling.

3. Fold over diagonally, slightly off centre.

4. Pull the sides together, using the cornflour and water paste to stick the two together.

5. Turn inside out by gently pushing the filled centre through the middle.

6. Heat enough oil in a wok for deep-fat frying and when hot, put in 4 of the filled wontons at a time. Cook until crisp and golden and remove to kitchen paper to drain. Repeat with the remaining filled wontons. Serve drizzled with honey.

Index